Nein.

Nein.

A Manifesto.
Eric Jarosinski

TEXT PUBLISHING MELBOURNE AUSTRALIA

textpublishing.com.au

The Text Publishing Company
Swann House
22 William Street
Melbourne Victoria 3000
Australia

Illustration of Theodor W. Adorno by Luc(as) de Groot
Trademark Eric Jarosinski, 2014
Cover design by Text

The Theodor W. Adorno quotation on the epigraph page is translated by Eric Jarosinski and is taken from a conversation between Adorno and Max Horkheimer in Horkheimer's collected works: "Diskussion über Theorie und Praxis," in Max Horkheimer, *Gesammelte Schriften, Nachgelassene Schriften 1949–1972.* S. Fischer 1989. The publisher is grateful to S. Fischer Verlage for permission to quote.

Some material from the Afterword originally appeared in different form in the author's article "#failedintellectual" in the *Chronicle of Higher Education.*

First published in the USA by Black Cat, an imprint of Grove Atlantic
Published in Australia in 2015 by The Text Publishing Company

Printed in Australia by Griffin Press, an Accredited ISO AS/NZS 14001:2004 Environmental Management System printer.

ISBN: 9781925240382
eISBN: 9781925095999

This book is printed on paper certified against the Forest Stewardship Council® Standards. Griffin Press holds FSC chain-of-custody certification SGS-COC-005088. FSC promotes environmentally responsible, socially beneficial and economically viable management of the world's forests.

FSC
www.fsc.org
MIX
Paper from
responsible sources
FSC® C009448

A former Ivy League professor, Eric Jarosinski is an expert on modern German literature, culture and critical thought. His Twitter feed, @NeinQuarterly, has more than 100,000 followers in more than 100 countries. Jarosinski and his work have been featured in numerous international publications, including the *New Yorker, Paris Review, Frankfurter Allgemeine Zeitung, Der Spiegel, Wall Street Journal, Slate* and *Irish Times.*

"The pleasure of thinking—
it cannot be recommended."
—Theodor W. Adorno

Contents

Introduction   xi

1. **Nein** is not no. Nein is not yes.
   Nein is nein.   1

2. **Nein** believes in nothing. Militantly.   11

3. **Nein** does not take questions.   23

4. **Nein** regrets to inform you.   35

5. **Nein** is not the medium.
   Nein is not the message.   47

6. **Nein** does not thank you for shopping.   61

7. **Nein** is not style. Nein is not syntax.   75

8. **Nein** says no. To a yes. That is a no.   91

9. **Nein** closes its eyes to your surveillance
   state. Your dating profile. Your blog.
   And hears the sea.   101

Glossary   115

Afterword   130

Introduction

It's not hard to say no. It's hard
to say it right. At the right time.
For the right reasons.

Harder still to keep saying it, especially
when we live in a world of yes. A tyranny
of yes.

Yes to family. Yes to friends. Yes to terms.
Yes to conditions. Yes to work. Yes to play.
Yes to a life of yes, yes, and yes, please.

But there is another life. An uncertain life.
It sings a song to no. Of no. For no.

Not just any no, however. A no of not
now. Not yet. And not only.

The no of Nein.

.

1. Nein is not no. Nein is not yes. Nein is nein.

#KeepItSimple

Only two problems with the world today.

---

1. The world.

And 2. Today.

Three, if you count tomorrow.

#TheFinePrint

Someday we will read the terms.

We will read the conditions.

We will wonder why we ever agreed to them.

And check yes.

#TheAudacityOfHope

The good news:

Our lost hope has been found.

The bad news:

It refuses to return.

#TheoryOfSocialMedia

Joy.

Found online.

In almost filling the emptiness.

Created online.

#SpinControl

Yes, world.

Truly.

You disgust me.

Please continue.

#SystemError

My God: dead.

My document: saved.

My prose: tired.

My screen: refreshed.

#BitterSchön

It's not the depression.

It's the anxiety.

The thought of waking up some morning.
Alone.

With nothing left to fear.

#GoldenRatios

My hope: half lost.

My poetry: half found.

My glass: half empty.

My grave: half full.

2. Nein believes in nothing. Militantly.

#LostAndFound

Lost: a pipe.
Found: art.

Lost: syllables.
Found: poetry.

Lost: religion.
Found: belief.

Lost: meaning.
Found: philosophy.

#UtopianNegation

Despair.

Seeking to find a better world.

And hope.

That it never will.

#Nihilisnt

1. Read Nietzsche.

2. Watch God die.

3. Re-read Nietzsche.

4. Watch nothing rise from the dead.

#God

He lived, they say.

Like he died.

As just another philosophy.

Killed by just another philosopher.

#FAQ

Ontology: what the fuck?

Causality: why the fuck?

Epistemology: how the why the fuck?

Phenomenology: the fuck.

#PhilosophyMadeEasy

---

1. Think.

---

2. Think.

---

3. Major in philosophy.

---

4. Ask yourself what you were thinking.

#SomethingForNothing

Ideology critique:

Everything is a construct.

Advanced ideology critique:

So is nothing.

#TruthOrDare

Art: The lie that tells the truth.

Art History: The truth about the lie.

Aesthetics: The truth of the lie.

Philosophy: The truth.

#Leftovers

Too Freudian for Jung.

Too Hegelian for Hegel.

Too old for Žižek.

Too cool for Frankfurt School.

#ReadingList

In spring: Proust. In Paris.

In summer: Kerouac. On the road.

In fall: Sontag. In New York.

In winter: Dostoyevsky. In a cold wind.
And a thin coat.

3. Nein does not take questions.

#DefiningTerms

Yes, there's a distinction.

Between negation and nihilism.

But 1. It's false.

And 2. It doesn't matter.

#OrderOfOperations

The poetry of negation.

Or the negation of poetry.

The inversion of cliché.

Or the cliché of inversion.

#CloseReading

Perhaps Marx is best read as religion.

Freud as literature.

Woolf as economics.

And Nietzsche as Nietzsche.

#SelfKnowledge

Everything you always wanted to know
about ideology:

But were afraid to ask.

Everything you always wanted to know
about epistemology:

But couldn't.

#TrialAndError

In fall: Read Kafka.

In winter: Understand Kafka.

In spring: Fall in love with Kafka.

In summer: Forget Kafka on the beach.

#AskingPrice

Question authority.

Become an authority.

Question yourself.

Ask your authority
if questioning is right for you.

#DidacticalMaterialism

Contradictions:

Have to be learned.

-Ologies:

Are usually taut.

#AllsQuiet

A moment of silence.

Observed solemnly.

For the unimaginable.

By the unspeakable.

#AutoGenesis

In the beginning:

There was the word.

And it was autocorrected.

To world.

4. Nein regrets to inform you.

#HowToFindHappiness

Think of where you last saw it.

See if it's still there.

If it's not, ask yourself why it left.

If it is, ask yourself why you didn't stay.

#Formulaic

Comedy = tragedy + time.

Dark comedy = tragedy + time + tragedy.

German comedy = tragedy + time − comedy.

Dark German Comedy = Greek tragedy.

#MultipleChoice

A. True.

B. False.

C. True until proven false.

D. False once proven true.

#MixedReception

The good news:

Technology has brought us closer together.

The bad news:

Please see above.

#GrandTheft

The poets stole love. From the lovers.

The lovers stole poetry. From the poets.

And the philosophers stole love
and poetry and philosophy.

From the philosophers.

#SweetBrokenDreams

The bad news:

Dreams don't come true.

The worse news:

Yours might.

#RhymeAndReason

Prose + deletion = poetry.

Poetry + deletion = good poetry.

Poetry + deletion + deletion = haiku.

Deletion + deletion + deletion = good
haiku.

#Howl

The greatest thoughts of my generation:

Destroyed by fragmentation.

The greatest fragmented thoughts of my generation:

Destroyed by completion.

#PeerReview

Marx: right.

History: wrong.

Foucault: disciplined.

Power: unpunished.

5. Nein is not the medium. Nein is not the message.

#GenreTrouble

The aphorism:

Philosophy's ship in literature's bottle.

The epigram:

Literature's hole in philosophy's bucket.

#MediaTheory

Another beautiful day.

For the medium.

Another existential crisis.

For the message.

#AufDeutsch

Millions of words.

In German.

For Doppelgänger.

Each of them identical.

#AestheticTheory

At least there's art.

Always there to remind us that
the world is full of beauty.

And it's very sorry:

But there's no room for any more.

#GermanEngineering

Yes, German words are long.

They were designed to minimize awkward silences.

But failed.

#HardCopy

No.

Print is not a waste of paper.

But yes.

A waste of words.

#AllTheoryIsLocal

Let's be honest:

It's all politics.

The rest is aesthetics.

Which is also politics.

#Hermenotics

Telling a tale full of sound and fury:

Idiot-proof.

Signifying nothing:

Harder than it looks.

#ThisIsNotAJoke

Magritte walks into a bar.

Smoking a pipe.

Sits down next to Freud.

Smoking a phallus.

#UnderArrest

A gentle reminder:

Nothing is ever lost in translation.

It's in hiding.

Negotiating terms of surrender.

#SocialMediation

So many bottles.

So few messages.

So many friends.

So few friends.

#Optics

Art: This is not a pipe.

Politics: This is not a lie.

The politics of art: This lie is not a lie.

The art of politics: Put this lie in your pipe.
But don't smoke it.

6. Nein does not thank you for shopping.

#HauntingEurope

Marx, Marxist, and Post-Marxist
walk into a bar.

Marx hates the prices.

Marxist hates the crowd.

Post-Marxist hates Marx.

#SaveTheReceipt

_____

Thank you for shopping at Nietzsche's.

_____

Please no eternal returns.

_____

Thank you for shopping at Freud's.

_____

Have a nice dad.

#CallMeFeuerbach

Thank you for calling the philosophers.

We're busy at the moment interpreting the world.

If you're calling to change it, please stay on the line.

The Revolution will be with you soon.

#Priceless

No, my dear commodity.

What we have is fetishization.

It's love.

Without the ideology.

#RetailNietzsche

Without fear.

Without hope.

Without remorse.

Thus shopped Zarathustra.

#ConsumerConfidences

It's not you.

It's your brand.

It's not me.

It's my demographic.

#WellRed

Radical: my reading of Marx.

Reactionary: your reading of Marx.

Revisionist: their reading of Marx.

Realistic:
none of us has ever actually read Marx.

#Weltanschauung

A gentle reminder:

To be thankful for the big things.

To fetishize the little things.

And to gently Photoshop
everything in between.

#LastCall

Marx, Engels, and the Proletariat
walk into a bar.

Marx drinks. Engels buys.
The Proletariat loses its chains.

Then its keys. Then its phone.

Then its Marx. Then its Engels.

#PistolsOrSabers

At least there are the radicals.

Always there to challenge our worldview.

To a bloody duel. At dawn.

Followed by brunch.

#ArrangeYourDesires

_____

By those you've yet to satisfy.

_____

Those you've yet to abandon.

_____

Those you'll never satisfy.

_____

And those you'll never satisfy until abandoned.

#NegationOfTheNegation

No, friends.

You don't have to suffer from false
consciousness –

To be a bourgeois academic Marxist.

But it helps.

7. Nein is not style. Nein is not syntax.

#SoundShifts

Living languages: sentenced to death.

Dead languages: writing us off.

Romance languages: losing their charm.

Computer languages: getting into poetry.

#RhetoricalAnswers

Parataxis: gin and tonic.

Catachresis: gin and tunic.

Catharsis: gin. No tonic.

Paratactical cathartic catachresis:
gin and gin. No tunic.

#HowToReadABook

Read what's written.

Ask how.

Read what's not written.

Wonder why.

#EvilTongues

Please:

Pardon our language.

It does not speak well of us.

This, our most original sin.

#FaultyTowers

Italian: the language of romance.

French: the language of love.

German: the love of language.

English: the love of English.

#TheoryOfLanguage

A wonder:

That we can communicate at all.

And if I've understood you correctly:

A curse.

#DeferredSentence

My French:

Pardoned.

My langue:

Out on parole.

#InvisibleInk

German.

It's for that sublime beauty.

For which there is a secret grammar.

But no words.

#PleaseListenCarefully

To report a stolen line, please press 1.

To report a lost poem, please press 2.

For a found poem, please press 3:

And hear these options again.

#WritingOnTheWall

Somewhere Magritte is in his studio.

Sitting quietly at his desk.

Reading de Saussure.

While smoking a painting.

#GloatingSignifiers

The poets remember it.

A time when words meant something.

Something important.

For which there are no words.

#ArrangeYourWords

By those that seduced you.

Those that betrayed you.

Those that cut you.

And those that comforted you.
And remained unsaid.

#ThePortableNietzsche

I give you my word:

Your own.

Personal.

Dead God.

8. Nein says no. To a yes. That is a no.

#StatusUpdate

My God: dead.

My dissertation: defended.

My degree: granted.

My debts: unforgiven.

#UtopianProjects

Say no to a nowhere.

And yes to a somewhere.

Somewhere else.

In the middle of nowhere.

#MultipleChoice

For the good news, please press 1.

For the bad news, please press 2.

For the very bad news, please try your call again tomorrow.

And press 1.

#JustLikeMe

Yes, we'll say.

Social media.

It's when our friends left our lives.

And moved into our phones.

#Breaking

In local news: what you already know.

World news: what you don't want to know.

Business news: what you don't understand.

But already know.

#PathToWisdom

---

1. True or false.

---

2. Truth or beauty.

---

3. Sturm und Drang.

---

4. False.

#DisciplineAndPunish

Philosophy: no truth.

History: no certainty.

Philosophy of history: no angel.

Philosophy of art history: no jobs.

#ErrorMessage

History will show that philosophy was mistaken.

Philosophy will show that history was mistaken.

And theory will show that theory was correct.

When mistaken.

9. Nein closes its eyes to your surveillance state. Your dating profile. Your blog. And hears the sea.

#LogicOfNegation

Yes.

There's a reason for the way things are.

But no.

Not a very good one.

#MyHegelianValentine

Logic: yes or no.

Dialectics: yes and no.

The dialectical logic of love: yes, then yes
or no, then yes.

And no.

#Daffodils

A lonely cloud:

Please alert the poets.

A lonely poet:

Please send in the clouds.

#Spring

Thoughts turn to love.

Love turns to poetry.

Poetry turns to philosophy.

Philosophy turns to philosophy. And falls
in love.

#TheUniversalLanguage

I just typed some arrows.

Numbers.

And various punctuation marks.

To say I love you.

#SelectiveAffinities

Philosophy:

The love of wisdom.

Loving a philosopher:

A poor life decision.

#SelfHelp

Own your alienation.

Commodify your disgust.

Deconstruct your despair.

Eat. Negate. Love.

#ArrangeYourBooks

By those that taught you love.

Those that taught you true love.

Those that taught you the love of books.

And those that taught you if love is ever
true, it's in books.

#PlatonicIdeals

There are those who love reading
philosophy.

Those who really love reading philosophy.

And those who really read philosophy.

And never love again.

#AufWiedersomething

A world without turmoil.

Without poverty.

Without injustice.

Without us.

#TheEnd

Patience, friends.

Change is slow.

The struggle long.

And Rome did not burn in a day.

Glossary

Adorno: German for YOLO.

Aesthetics: Art for the artless.

Analytic philosophy:
When mathematicians try their hand at poetry.

Anxiety: Fear of the unknown.
(**Depression:** Fear of the known.)

Aphorisms: 1. Old ships in new bottles.
2. Philosophy for those with little Zeit.
Written by those with little Geist.

Art: The silence of the ancient mariner's painted
ship. Upon Coleridge's painted ocean.

Art history: The study of art without art.
And history without history.

Atheism: A religion without a prayer.

Benjamin, Walter: The mourning
of philosophy cut short by history.

Book: A relic of the days when paper
was wasted on words.

Borges: Argentina's greatest German author.

Brunch: The one thing everyone believes in on Sunday.

Capitalism: The ship of state rigged by pirates. (**Communism:** The ship of state rigged by the state.)

Change: What you want. When, where, and how you do not want it.

Close reading: The art of reading what has never been written in order to write a book that will never be read.

Coffee: The diuretic of enlightenment.

Cold War: A conflict too expensive to be fought, but too cheap for a Roman numeral.

Commodity fetishism: Mistaking someone's labor for something you would want to buy.

Consumption: Capitalism's drug of choice.

Continental philosophy: What Europe does when it's depressed.

Craigslist: A casual encounter with the social contract.

Culture: The cigarette not smoked after not having sex.

Cynicism: The hope that someday you will have known better all along.

Dead certainty: Socrates without a question.

Deconstruction: Reading with a microscope. Thinking with a hammer. And writing with an erasure.

Degree: Devised by doctors to take one's temperature or tuition.

Dialectics: A Werner Herzog documentary narrated by Klaus Kinski.

Diplomacy: The art of turning swords into plowshares. Plowshares into tractors. And tractors into tanks.

Discretion: An undertaker who never says die.

Elegy: Pathos played in a minor key.

Emoticon: Symbol expressing an emotion we can no longer express in the form of a face we can no longer countenance.

English: A language everybody speaks but nobody can spell.

Ethics: Curiosity killed by a cat.

Europe: A continent tied to the left that drifts to the right.

Failed intellectual: One who tries to intellectualize one's failure. And fails. At times brilliantly.

Foreign policy: The logical extension of illogical domestic policies.

Frankfurt School: An institute that taught us to read Freud like Marx. Marx like Hegel. And Adorno like Adorno.

French: A language invented for making love, but used to make cheese, revolution, and philosophy.

French theory: Americans who still smoke.

Freudian slip: When the unconscious speaks in tongues.

Fundamentalism: A literal misreading of the misunderstood.

Genius: When sadness speaks to loneliness. And laughs.

German: A language invented for philosophy but used to build automobiles.

German beer: Carefully brewed in accordance with purity, and slowly poured in defiance of gravity.

German literature: Where protagonists go to die.

God: 1. A deity who looks like Marx, was pronounced dead by Nietzsche, and envied by Freud. 2. The monster over our beds.

GOP: An American political party devoted to the principle of one nation under God. And one above.

Graduate school: Related fields seeking advanced degrees of separation.

Grammar: IKEA assembly instructions that are different in every country. But only available in German.

Happiness: A feeling of well-being appreciated once it has stopped.

Hegel: A philosopher best understood if never read.

Hermeneutics: The science of reading text messages. (**Critical Hermeneutics:** The art of deleting them.)

Hipster: Indifference wasted on the young.

History: The victors' present for the vanquished.

Hope: A beacon made of fog.

Humanism: The sober realization that we're all we've got.

Ideology: The mistaken belief that your beliefs are neither beliefs nor mistaken.

Instability: When capital is frightened by its own shadow.

Instagram: A marketplace in which pictures of your cat are exchanged for a thousand unspoken words of derision.

Internet, the: A network of cables, wires, and tubes connecting us all. To cables. Wires. And tubes.

Joyce: A stream of whiskey that has traded clarity for consciousness.

Justice: A stick disguised as a carrot.

Kafka: A law under arrest.

Kitsch: The indifference that will always love you.

Life: A leading cause of death.

LinkedIn: A close-knit community of distant acquaintances who would like you to join in the fun of finding a job.

Lobbying: Buying influence from those selling affluence.

Logic: A multiple-choice question that is A. True or B. False.

Lottery: A round-trip ticket from delusion to grandeur.

Love: 1. A temporary truce between indifference and disgust. 2. A second that charges by the hour. 3. The comfort found in knowing that at least one other person has judgment as poor as your own.

Marriage: A union of two souls. On strike.

Marxism: The balding theories of the bearded.

Melancholy: When a dash of disappointment renders an etching of sadness.

Metaphor: Just another word. For just another word. (**Simile:** The metaphor's, like, less articulate cousin.)

Mid-life crisis: The sudden realization that you've been dying all along.

Morality: The damned damning their damnedest.

Morning: Something that can never be fixed once it's been broken.

Nabokov: A collector of butterflies who releases them as paragraphs.

Nationalism: The fallible notion of an infallible nation.

Negotiation: The art of making a turn of phrase sound like a change of heart.

Nietzsche: A poet with a philosophy. A system without a method. A mustache with a man.

Nihilism: The idealistic notion that nothing can change the world.

Nothing: Everything you always wanted. But less.

NSA: An American intelligence agency devoted to protecting the world from privacy.

Online dating: Your last best hope of finding people like you who don't like people like you.

Patriotism: The love of country by those who've never left it.

Peace: What everybody's fighting for.

Performance art: Six Doppelgängers in Search of a Selfie.

Philosophy: The love of wisdom befalling those seduced by their own.

Poet: One who breaks lines to complete a thought.

Poetry: The fullest expression of language's forbidden desire to die alone.

Politics: A Greek tragedy set in Italy. (**Political rhetoric:** Smoke that can't look itself in the mirror.)

Postmodernism: Never meeting a cat you didn't already know from the Internet.

Praxis: Word used in theory to avoid it in practice.

Profit: A dog that runs away from the poor and returns to the rich.

Progress: A drone afraid of flying.

Prose: Poetry without the poetry. (**Poetry:** Prose without the punctuation.)

Psychoanalysis: Smoking your father's cigar. On your mother's couch.

Pun: A small change to a word reflecting a far larger error in judgment.

Quip: A joke told in tweed.

Religion: A set of beliefs about why yours are wrong.

Rhetoric: The art of saying what people don't want to hear in a way they wish they'd said.

Romance: The French art of living a long life of small deaths.

Romantic comedy: A sad movie in love with the box office.

Science: The art of method.

Selfie: A portrait of someone we used to know. Taken by someone we used to respect.

Semiotics: The study of how meaning is made to be misunderstood.

Smart phone: A device designed for working too late and dying too soon.

Social media: 1. A technology for following those you don't want to lead and befriending those you don't want to know. 2. A gated community of ideas.

Society: A system of errors.

Spanish: A language spoken by Cervantes. In a story written by Borges.

Sunday: A day kept holy by sleeping off spirits.

Tattoo: A permanent and predictable statement about one's dynamic individualism.

Technology: The deepest abyss on the flattest of screens.

Theology: A field devoted to writing the unreadable about knowing the unknowable.

Theory: A branch of philosophy and comparative literature devoted to disregarding both.

Time: Wasted space.

Today: A present nobody wants. But can never return.

Tomorrow: What we always want to see. Until we do.

Translation: The art of losing trees in a forest.

Transparency: A clear demonstration of that which remains clearly hidden.

Truth: 1. That which nobody wants but everybody has. 2. A love song in German sung by a drunken Russian sailor.

Tweet: Both a noun and a verb for a text that is both too short and too long.

Twitter: Attention Spam.

Wanderlust: A sudden desire to be stuck in traffic.

Weekend: The two days of the week when your alienation is all your own.

Žižek: 1. A Slovenian passing as a Stalinist. 2. Lacan without a mirror.

Afterword

This little book is the result of a rather spectacular failure. While struggling to write an academic tome, one I hoped might help me get tenure at an Ivy League research university, I discovered Twitter. In large measure this would prove to be the end of not only the project I had been working on for so long, but of my academic career as a whole. It was also the start of a strange new occupation as what I've termed an Internet aphorist, though I still have difficulty defining exactly what the job entails.

Having never been one for blogs or social media, I was singularly unimpressed with Twitter when first introduced. Yet I soon found its 140-character limit, relative anonymity, and the escape it seemed to offer from the isolation of academic life extremely liberating. I invented a fictitious journal—*Nein. Quarterly: A Compendium of Utopian Negation*—and began developing an online persona based on Theodor W. Adorno, one of the philosophers I'd been struggling to write about in my book. For better or worse, from that point on my days were spent ignoring the ticking of the tenure clock while writing jokes and aphorisms about philosophy, art, language, and literature.

What's emerged in the few years that have followed, apart from unemployment, is a perspective that is misanthropic yet romantic, authoritative yet absurd, principled yet darkly nihilistic. In short, I found a voice that is both invented yet somehow more authentic than that hiding behind the tortured qualifiers and anxious hedging of my academic work. And to my surprise, it spoke to others as well, gradually finding real resonance and a highly diverse global audience.

My accomplishments to date have been modest, yet they might well mean more to me than my abandoned book project ever could have: some people are learning German, reading Kafka, or studying philosophy who might not have otherwise; in my work online and in European newspapers I've been able to represent a somewhat alternative, self-critical American perspective abroad; and I'd like to think that a depressing joke about cultural pessimism and despair has occasionally managed to brighten someone's day.

It is no exaggeration to say that I owe thousands of people thanks, both online and off, for the kindness that has made this venture possible. Despite the apparent bleakness of my work, I'd like to think that some sense of that spirit of generosity has managed to survive within it. Kafka is quoted as having said that there is always hope—just not for us. In its own little way, this book seeks to second that.